D1516341

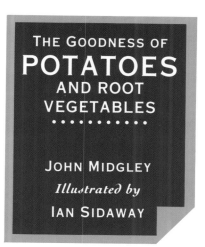

THE GOODNESS OF
POTATOES
AND ROOT VEGETABLES
· · · · · · · · · ·

JOHN MIDGLEY

Illustrated by

IAN SIDAWAY

RANDOM HOUSE
NEW YORK

ACKNOWLEDGEMENTS

The author thanks Sue Midgley and Jo Swinnerton
for kindly checking the text, and R. Griffiths of
the Potato Marketing Board for useful information
about potato varieties.
He thanks Sri Owen for her kind permission to borrow
a recipe from her book,
Indonesian Food and Cookery
(Prospect Books).

FURTHER READING

For those interested in reading more about food and health
The Food Pharmacy, by Jean Carper (Simon and Schuster)
and *Superfoods*, by Michael Van Straten and Barbara Griggs
(Dorling Kindersley) are recommended. Harold McGee's
On Food and Cooking (Harper Collins) and Reay Tannahill's
Food in History (Penguin) are also highly recommended.

Published in the United States by Random House, Inc., New York.

This work was originally published in Great Britain by
Pavilion Books Limited, London.

Library of Congress Cataloging-in-Publication Data

Midgley, John.
The goodness of potatoes and other roots/John Midgley;
illustrated by Ian Sidaway.
p. cm. – (The Goodness of)
ISBN 0-679-41625-0
1. Cookery (Potatoes) 2. Potatoes – utilization. 3. Potatoes –
Health aspects. I. Title. II. Series: Midgley, John. Goodness of.
TX803.P8M54 1992
641.6'521 – dc20 92-13766

Manufactured in Belgium

2 4 6 8 9 7 5 3

First U.S. edition

CONTENTS
· · · · · · · · · · ·

PART ONE

ROOTS AND TUBERS
· · · · · · · · · ·

There is an essential difference between potatoes and other tubers, and true root vegetables. Potatoes, Jerusalem artichokes (root artichokes), sweet potatoes, yams, taro and manioc (cassava) are tubers, which are defined as 'underground structures consisting of a solid, thickened, rounded outgrowth of a stem or rhizome, bearing eyes or buds from which new plants may arise'. So, a single tuber gives rise to several plants. By contrast, root vegetables such as beetroot, (beet), carrots, swedes (rutabaga), turnips, parsnips, radishes, and celeriac (celery root) are the swollen subterranean stems of plants from which the leaves sprout, so each vegetable is the root of a single plant. Despite this subtle difference, roots and tubers tend to be bracketed and share certain broad similarities in their cooking characteristics. They are all nutritious, and perhaps none more so than the potato.

Once considered fit only for animal fodder, the potato (*solanum tuberosum*) has become an essential starchy staple in many parts of the world, notably in central and northern Europe, North America and in the British Isles and Eire. It belongs to the same group of plants as nightshade, is hardy in most climates, and extremely versatile in cookery. Its culinary uses are many, as it can be puréed, deep fried, sautéed, baked, roasted and boiled. It is also an essential ingredient in many soups and salads (in Russia and Poland potatoes are also used to distil vodka). Much of this diversity is reflected in the recipes in this book.

The hundreds of potato varieties are classified as either 'new' or 'main crop'. The former are harvested while the leaves are still green and are smaller and sweeter with very thin, flaky skins. They have a waxy texture, and so keep their shape particularly well after boiling, and are perfect in salads.

New potatoes cultivated in the UK generally come to market in two batches, the first appearing from June to July, the second from July to August, but imports are available much earlier.

Some new potato varieties

Aminca	International	Nadine
Ausonia	Kidney	Nicola
Caribe	Jemseg	Pentland Javelin
Carlingford	Jersey Royal	Red Nordland
Catriona	Linzer	Red Pontiac
Charlotte	Delicatess	Red la Rouge
Duke of York	Marfona	Red la Soda
Fundy	Maris Bard	Sieglinde
Home Guard	Maris Peer	Spunta

Main croppers are a much larger group and are available from August through to October, then stored throughout the winter months. These varieties are harvested after the foliage has withered and the tubers have developed into mature potatoes, with harder, set skins. They are immensely varied and behave in markedly different ways when cooked.

Some main crop potato varieties

Arcadia Russet	Kerr's Pink	Record
Ailsa	King Edward	Red Desirée
Alpha	Maris Piper	Romano
Atlantic	Monona	Roseval
Belle de	Norchip	Russet Burbank
Fontenay	Penta	Sebago
Bintje	Pentland Dell,	Shepody
Cara	Hawk, Ivory,	Superior
Chieftain	and Squire	Wauseon
Estima	Pink Fir Apple	White Rose
Golden Wonder	Raritan	Yukon Gold
Kennebec	Ratte	

In general, floury, starchy potatoes, including Ailsa, Catriona, Golden Wonder, Marfona, Maris Piper, Penta, the Pentland varieties of Dell, Hawk, Ivory and Squire, Record and Russet Burbank are best suited to baking, roasting and frying.

Firm, waxy potatoes are best for boiling and salads, among them Aminca, Belle de Fontenay, Carlingford, Charlotte, International Kidney, Linzer Delicatess, Maris Bard and Maris Peer, Pentland Javelin, Pink Fir Apple, Ratte, Roseval and Sieglinde. These keep their shape well.

Among the best general-purpose potatoes are the varieties Cara, Red Desirée, Estima, Home Guard, Kerr's Pink, King Edward, Penta and Spunta, although in general it is best to stick to the waxy new crop varieties for salad use.

The principal British crops are of the varieties Maris Piper, Estima, Pentland Squire, Cara and Record. Of the sixty or so North American and Canadian varieties, the Russet Burbank is the standard potato for french fries and, indeed, McDonalds restaurants around the world use this large, heavy tuber to guarantee consistency of quality. Baking is the favourite American method of cooking potatoes to which the popular Russet Burbank is perfectly suited. There are four potato harvests in North America, corresponding to the seasons: the largest takes place in the northern states in the fall; a winter harvest comes from Florida; a spring harvest from California and Arizona, and one in the summer months, from Michigan, Virginia, California and Texas.

It is encouraging to observe the admirable progress that has been made by the supermarket chains in re-introducing older varieties with interesting flavours, such as the white-skinned Catriona, the salmon-coloured Kerr's Pink and the slender, knobbly Pink Fir Apple, first introduced in 1900. By stocking up to forty or so different varieties in a given year, they have been instrumental also in promoting a much greater awareness of the many different varieties of potato as high-quality, gourmet foods that reward experimentation in cookery.

Potatoes should always be removed from their plastic bags as soon as possible, to prevent spoiling, and should be stored in a cool, dry place, never in the fridge or the starch will convert to sugar. Two toxic conditions affecting potatoes should be avoided: any potatoes with greenish skins should be discarded, and any sprouting eyes should be cut out.

Other tubers

The other important edible tubers are the sweet potato (*ipomoea batatas*), a convolvulus plant native to Central America, cassava, or manioc (*manihot utilissima*), the Jerusalem, or root artichoke (*helianthus tuberosus*), the yam (*dioscorea batatas*), and the taro (*colocasia antiquorum*). With the exception of the Jerusalem artichoke, these are indispensable staples for hundreds of thousands of people in tropical countries in both hemispheres and a major source of dietary carbohydrate.

Native to North America, Jerusalem artichokes are the most suitable tubers for the average kitchen gardener as they require little attention, are hardy and occupy less space than potatoes. Planted in a row in early spring, they will be ready for harvesting in the autumn, when the foliage is already dying back. The stems should be cut and the tubers dug up, as required. (They can be stored in the soil throughout the winter.) Once planted, they should be trained vertically on to stakes. If any tubers are left behind, they will produce new plants in the spring.

Root vegetables

Perhaps the most popular of all root vegetables is the carrot (*daucus carota*), which is believed to be native to Europe. Although not a staple food, it is an exceptionally nutritious and surprisingly versatile vegetable that is held in virtually universal esteem, both raw and cooked. Carrots are an ideal winter salad ingredient, make delicious and colourful soups, an excellent side dish, a healthy juice, delightful stir-fries, and can even be baked to make a moist, spicy cake. They are available throughout the year but the new crops appearing in early summer are sweetest and most succulent. Look out especially for baby carrots, which are best appreciated raw or lightly boiled and glazed in a very little butter, with plenty of fresh mint and parsley, or with brown sugar and cinnamon. The old wives' tale that carrot eaters are endowed with enhanced night vision is false, yet the orange colour betrays a high level of beta carotene, a powerful cancer-suppressing substance found also in green leaf vegetables. People who eat very large quantities may actually turn a jaundiced orange colour, especially on the palms of the hands, an effect also promoted by eating large quantities of orange-coloured citrus fruits. Other than presenting an alarming appearance, the effect appears to be innocuous. However, it is never sensible to over-indulge in any single food, and even relatively small amounts (as little as one carrot a day, for example) are believed by some doctors to offer protection against cancers of the lung, oesophagus, pancreas and larynx.

Interestingly, orange carrots were developed relatively recently by Dutch plant breeders. Until the seventeenth century, carrots were black, white and purple, and black and white carrot varieties are still grown, especially in the United States, France and Italy. The varieties divide into three groups: round, stubby, and the ubiquitous long, tapering carrots.

Carrots are easy to grow and will provide a continuous crop if sown in stages throughout the year. Seeds should be sown in rows and later thinned, and the soil kept reasonably moist. Carrot fly poses the only real threat, but this can be discouraged if onions are planted near by.

Closely related to the carrot and also native to Europe is the parsnip (*pastinaca sativa*). Like the carrot, it comes in squat and tapering varieties, is sweet-tasting and can be grown at most times of the year, but is definitely best after the first frosts of the year have enhanced its flavour. It is thus a useful food at a time

when other fresh vegetables are scarce. Being hardy and requiring little attention, this root is quite rewarding to grow, although it takes almost a year to harvest from the time the seeds are sown, and so ties up valuable soil space for a long period. It is especially good roasted, fried or puréed and makes delicious soups.

Although it has long been appreciated in continental Europe, and especially in France where it is known as *céleri-rave*, celeriac, or celery root (*apium graveolens* var. *rapaceum*), is fast becoming fashionable in Britain. It is a variety of the celery plant, with the same strong, peppery flavour and is grown especially

for its swollen root. Less trouble to grow than common celery because it does not need to be blanched, it is none the less difficult unless sown from seed in March and planted out in full sun, in rich, warm soil, no earlier than late May. A winter vegetable, celeriac is harvested from late October onwards. Sweet young roots are preferable to old woody ones but they are only worth lifting when properly swollen. They are best peeled and grated and eaten raw, or lightly blanched, puréed, baked in a gratin, or made into soups.

The turnip (*brassica rapa*) and swede, or rutabaga (*brassica napobrassica*) are both native to Europe and members of the cabbage family. Turnips come in several varieties, varying in size, shape and colour. The peak season varies from country to country, but spring should see the first British crops in the shops, although French imports arrive a little earlier. Turnips grow quickly, can be sown in rows in full sun as soon as the danger of frosts has past and are harvested within 3 to 4 months. Small roots are pleasant when glazed like carrots, added to rich stews, or puréed. Swedes are larger, with coarse skins. Swedes need open sites such as fields to grow successfully and are therefore an unsuitable garden vegetable. With their strong flavour of cabbage and yellowish flesh, they are best puréed, with or without potatoes, and well seasoned with black pepper and nutmeg, or cut up and added to stews and casseroles. They have long been integral to the peasant cooking of northern Europe and are a valuable winter-cropping vegetable.

It is the cuisines of northern, central and eastern Europe and the Balkans more than any others, that make best use of sweet-tasting beetroot, or beet (*beta vulgaris*). This root vegetable is related to a wild Mediterranean seashore plant called *beta maritima* and is widely eaten (cooked, not raw) as a salad ingredient, in soups (the most famous being Ukrainian borscht and Polish barsch), and as a pickle. Although cooked beetroot is readily available, it is worth looking out for fresh roots, which are a dusty pinkish brown in colour. Soups should be attempted only with fresh beetroot. The many varieties can be globe or long-rooted, including one that is golden. Beetroot are well worth growing, not just for the roots but also for the sleek, red-ribbed leaves. They should be sown in rich soil in spring, thinned and pulled while the root is still small.

Radishes (*raphanus sativus*) are an ancient root vegetable that is widely distributed around the globe. The many different varieties range from the common small red and white radishes, elongated and round in shape, to more exotic specimens from the Far East such as the enormous Japanese daikon and the white winter radish, or mooli. Summer radishes taste peppery, occasionally hot, and are primarily eaten raw, as a salad vegetable. Winter radishes are larger roots that may also be eaten raw or cooked. Both summer and winter radishes are easy to grow: the former mature extremely quickly and are normally sown thinly in spring and summer, the latter are slower to grow and are sown in late summer.

Kohlrabi (*brassica oleracea*) is the odd man out in that it is not a true root vegetable. In fact, the edible turnip-like ball is a swollen stem that grows just above the surface. However, in all other respects kohlrabi are very similar to turnips. The vegetable is appreciated in Italy, France and Germany and in other central European countries, as well as in India, and is slowly becoming a little better known domestically. Varieties can be green- or purple-skinned and are very fast to grow, maturing within twelve weeks. Kohlrabi can be treated in the same way as turnips, or the leaves can be lightly boiled.

THE GOODNESS OF ROOTS AND TUBERS
· · · · · · · · · ·

Potatoes, carrots, beetroot, radishes, turnips, and sweet potatoes may well play an important role in the prevention of diseases and the promotion of general good health.

That a diet consisting mainly of potatoes kept Irish peasants healthy until the failure of the potato crop in 1845 suggests that they are a highly nutritious food. Potatoes are a starchy staple in northern Europe, the British Isles and North America, and starch is an essential component of the diet. Starch is present in most traditional diets around the world, be it in the form of rice, throughout Asia; maize, in the Americas; bread, in the Mediterranean and the Middle East; or tubers like yams, sweet potatoes and manioc, in many tropical countries in both hemispheres. Potatoes are rich in vitamin C, high in potassium, which is concentrated in and around the skins, and are also an excellent source of fibre. Vitamin C is essential to health and suspected of being a vital anti-carcinogenic substance. Without adequate fibre in the diet, diseases of the stomach and bowel, including the cancers that are an all too common cause of premature deaths in western society, present a far greater risk. Potato skins are especially nutritious as well as having antioxidant properties that are also important in cancer prevention and should be preserved wherever possible. (Main crop potatoes have harder skins, so new potatoes are the best varieties to use when boiling unpeeled potatoes.) Potassium is also effective in lowering blood pressure: a traditional remedy is a tea made from potato peelings, and potato juice is an old remedy for a variety of ailments, including arthritis and ulcers. A diet too heavy on potatoes is not recommended for diabetics, however, as it can raise blood sugar levels.

Carrots and beetroot have attracted medical attention for the apparently powerful anti-cancer properties

of beta carotene and beet juice. Experiments on animals and tests on cigarette smokers and other high-risk groups have shown that beta carotene, found naturally in carrots and other orange-fleshed fruits and vegetables, including sweet potatoes, as well as dark green leaf vegetables blocks the pre-tumour stage of early cancer development and probably also retards the progress of existing tumours, when used in combination with conventional therapies such as radiation treatment.

Even more exciting are the antioxidant properties of substances found in these fruit and vegetables. They are now believed to have a wide range of beneficial effects, boosting the immune system, suppressing the disruption of cells, protecting the cardiovascular system and reducing inflammation. Beetroot has been used in anti-cancer therapy in Russia and eastern Europe. It is also valued as a general tonic, particularly for convalescents and anaemics.

Radishes are an ancient health food: the Greek historian Herodotus noted an inscription recording the amounts paid for the food – radishes, onions and garlic – that sustained the labourers who erected the pyramids. A member of the *cruciferae* family of vegetables, the radish is suspected of possessing cancer-blocking substances, as are its relatives, the turnip, the swede and the kohlrabi. At the time of going to press, American scientists have just announced the successful isolation of a chemical called sulforaphane that has demonstrated anti-cancer properties in animal tests. Other cruciferous plants are also good sources of sulforaphane, including cabbage, broccoli, Brussels sprouts, cauliflower, kale, spinach and some other dark green and yellow vegetables. The compound acts by accelerating the process of detoxification in the body, helping to block the formation of tumours by increasing the body's resistance to carcinogens. Although this has been shown in animal tests, laboratory tests on human cells have produced similar results.

The edible green leaves of radishes, turnips and kohlrabi are also rich in beta carotene. Turnips, although very high in water content are rich in vitamin C, and are a traditional remedy for gout, having the power to eliminate uric acid and purify the blood.

ETYMOLOGY

· · · · · · · · · ·

A relative of the sunflower, the Jerusalem artichoke is not named for any connection with the eponymous city. Rather, the name is a corruption of the Italian word for sunflower (*girasole* means 'turning to the sun'). The English, Spanish, Italian and Greek words for potato all derive from a Caribbean Indian word for the sweet potato, *batata*, that the Spaniards loosely applied to that tuber and to the true potato. The English, French and Italian names for carrot derive ultimately from Greek, via Latin *carota*, whereas, characteristically, the Spanish word *zanahoria* betrays an Arabic root. Kohlrabi is a German word meaning turnip-cabbage, which aptly describes the vegetable in question. Turnip derives from Old English *neep* (Latin *napus*), but the prefix is of unknown origin, although *Chambers Dictionary* hazards a possible derivation from French *tour*, meaning rounded. Swede is an abbreviation of 'Swedish turnip' (*brassica campestris* var. *rutabaga*), introduced into Scotland from Sweden c.1781. (Rutabaga was a dialect word meaning 'ram's foot'.) Radish derives from the Latin word for root, *radix*. Parsnip is a corruption of Latin *pastinaca*, joined to the Old English word *neep*.

ROOTS AND TUBERS IN HISTORY

'A Roman meal…
a radish and an egg.'
WILLIAM COWPER

Like so many other modern food plants, these vegetables are rooted in prehistory. The wild ancestors of edible roots and tubers were part of the diet of early man. Even on the fringes of the American ice sheet, the forerunners of manioc, yams and potatoes allowed early foragers to dig up nutritious food preserved from the cold air. In prehistoric Europe, wild turnips and radishes offered similar nutrition. By 3000 BC, Mesopotamian farmers cultivated crops of turnips and radishes with the aid of irrigation. Radishes were also a favourite food of the Egyptians, while beetroot and turnips were highly prized by the ancient Greeks. Carrots probably originated in Greece and were eaten by the Greeks and Romans, and are mentioned by Pliny. The Romans introduced their cultivation into other parts of Europe, along with turnips, beetroot, radishes and parsnips. These root vegetables were grown by monks in their kitchen gardens throughout the Dark and early Middle Ages to provide sustenance through the 200 or so meatless days of the year and were a crucial part of the medieval and later European diet. Writing in 1719, a Monsieur Misson remarked upon the Englishman's passion for roast and boiled beef served with 'heaps of cabbage, carrots, turnips or some other herbs or roots, well peppered and salted, and swimming in butter'. Further north, beetroot was an important crop that, to survive the long, dark winter, the Scandinavian farmer had to preserve in bulk by pickling. Dutch farmers were pioneers of the scientific approach to agriculture, and developed an intricate system of crop rotation that was copied in other countries. Under a simplified version of this system, grains for human consumption were

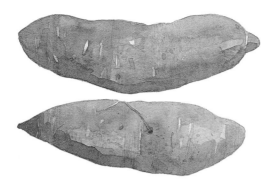

grown in rotation with turnips and other roots providing animal fodder.

Further afield, the Maoris brought yams and sweet potatoes on their epic sea migration to New Zealand, learned to grow them successfully in the unsuitable, temperate climate, and readily adopted the potato when this was eventually introduced by Europeans. For Hindus, kohlrabi and radishes have long been important components of a largely vegetarian diet, and Chinese farmers mastered the art of growing radishes and other root vegetables throughout the year by means of various devices designed to protect crops from cold.

Meanwhile, in the western hemisphere, the Peruvian Indians had acquired over 3000 years' experience of cultivating the potato. Its hardiness at cold Andean altitudes meant that it was the more resilient equivalent of maize, the starchy staple that was grown at lower levels by other Indian civilizations. In the Caribbean islands, the Spaniards discovered how the local Indian inhabitants relied on two tubers: the cassava, from which a very durable bread was made, and the sweet potato, the tuber of a tropical convolvulus.

The Spaniards adopted their word for the latter – *batatas* – and named the true potato after it when they first encountered specimens on reaching Peru. Here, they saw how the Indians had learned to preserve the potato by dehydrating it. This substance, known as *chuñu*, was a nourishing food which the conquering Spaniards fed to native silver miners. They used potatoes as basic rations aboard ships and soon started to cultivate them at home. Potatoes were introduced into Italy and other European countries from Spain, although Sir Francis Drake was responsible for their introduction to England, having acquired a consignment in the Colombian port of Cartagena. Although today potatoes are the most important source of starch in the diets of some western countries, they were by no means universally accepted save as animal fodder and sustenance for the very poorest peasants until some 200 years after their introduction, although in Ireland they were readily adopted by the majority of the population as the principal staple.

The popularity of potatoes in Ireland may have been because the crop was less vulnerable than grain to damage by marauding English soldiers, was high-yielding and therefore met the pressing need of the typical small holder to feed his family and animals, rather than to harvest cash crops. Such was the dependence of the Irish and, to a lesser extent, the Scottish rural populations on the potato that a succession of crop failures throughout Europe, caused by wind-borne spores of the potato blight fungus and exacerbated by a particularly cold, wet summer in 1845 – the year of the Great Famine – brought massive starvation and an outbreak of diseases caused by vitamin deficiency. Scurvy quickly erupted due to a lack of vitamin C, followed by symptoms of a deficiency of other vitamins that were normally supplied in cow's milk; with no potatoes to feed them, the family cows had to be slaughtered. The most far-reaching effect of these crop failures was the decision of many Irish and Scots peasants to emigrate to America. Although it grew wild as far as Colorado, the potato was introduced to North America over a century earlier by the first Irish settlers. Later, a second wave of Irish immigrants and Mormon farmers planted large crops in the states of Utah and Idaho and succeeded in popularizing the potato. Ever wider cultivation in the latter state has made its name synonymous with the tuber in America.

Today a new fascination with potatoes and their many varieties old and new will ensure that they will continue to be enjoyed as a nutritious food of some sophistication, enjoying a new elevated status that is a far cry from their former use as mere fodder. The following recipes for potatoes and root vegetables are inspired by the cooking traditions of different countries. Unless otherwise stated, they are intended to serve four.

PART
TWO

GNOCCHI DI PATATE
· · · · · · · · · · ·

Potato gnocchi are universally popular and not at all heavy. Starchy, floury varieties or general purpose, main crop potatoes will make good gnocchi. With a little practice, shaping them gets easier. The important thing is not to worry about perfect shapes but to enjoy their surprising lightness as vehicles for the sauce. Serve with either of the sauce recipes below, or with a meat *ragù*, or with any of the pesto recipes from *The Goodness of Olive Oil*.

675g/1½lb potatoes, peeled
2fl oz/4 tbs milk
1fl oz/2 tbs olive oil
½ tsp salt
450g/1lb/2½ cups plain (all-purpose) flour

Put the potatoes and plenty of water into a large pan and bring to a boil. Cover and boil the potatoes until they are cooked, about 20 minutes. Pour away the water, add the milk, olive oil and salt and quickly mash the potatoes with a hand masher until they are completely smooth.

Allow the mixture to cool a little, then combine it with most of the flour, kneading thoroughly with floured hands. Flour a work surface, break up the dough into smaller balls and roll these out into long snakes, about the width of your finger. Cut into 1½cm/⅔ inch squares, press them against a fork, dust lightly with flour and reserve them.

Prepare the sauce.

While the sauce is cooking, bring plenty of salted water to the boil in a very large pot. When it is boiling furiously, drop in the gnocchi. They will cook very quickly and may be removed with a slotted spoon as soon as they rise to the surface.

Combine thoroughly with the sauce in a heated bowl and serve with extra parmesan.

Gorgonzola sauce

200g/7oz gorgonzola cheese
110ml/4fl oz/$^{1}/_{2}$ cup milk
110ml/4fl oz/$^{1}/_{2}$ cup dry white wine
1 tsp salt
freshly milled black pepper
110g/4 oz piece of parmesan, grated

Dice the cheese and combine it with the remaining
ingredients in a small saucepan. Over a low heat, slowly melt the cheese, stirring occasionally. The sauce will
be ready in about 5 minutes. Serve with extra parmesan, to taste.

Tomato sauce

400g/14oz can of plum tomatoes, chopped
3 cloves of garlic, peeled and chopped
2fl oz/4 tbs extra virgin olive oil
salt
freshly milled black pepper
fresh basil leaves

Combine all the ingredients except the basil in a small saucepan and simmer for about 15 minutes. Tear up and add the basil. Serve.

Baked gnocchi

2 bags (each 150g/5oz) of Italian mozzarella cheese
1fl oz/2 tbs olive oil
crushed contents of a 400g/14oz can of plum tomatoes
2 cloves of garlic, peeled and finely chopped
2fl oz/4 tbs dry white wine
pinch of oregano
salt
freshly milled black pepper
110g/4oz piece of parmesan, grated

Pre-heat an oven to 220°C/425°F/gas mark 7.

Prepare gnocchi, following the basic recipe. Dice the mozzarella. Heat the olive oil in a small pan and add the tomatoes, garlic, white wine and oregano. Reduce over a medium heat for 4 minutes, then season and remove. Lightly oil a baking dish. In it, combine the full quantity of gnocchi with the tomato sauce, mozzarella and parmesan cheeses, mixing them well. Bake for 15–20 minutes.

GLAZED CARROTS

A very tasty accompaniment to any main course. Baby carrots especially are delicious glazed whole, and large, older carrots should be sliced into discs. After the water has boiled away, the carrots are briefly glazed in the residue of sugar and butter. Garnish with a generous quantity of mixed fresh green herbs, such as parsley or coriander (cilantro), and mint.

675g/1 1/2lb carrots, peeled
water
1 tsp salt
1 tsp sugar
50g/2oz butter
mixed fresh herbs, washed and chopped
freshly milled black pepper

Cut the carrots into sections, appropriate to their size and maturity. Put them in a pan with the salt, sugar and butter and just enough water barely to cover them. Bring to the boil and cook the carrots until the water has evaporated. (This will take about 10 minutes.) Let them brown a little in the pan, stirring constantly. Transfer to a heated serving bowl, mix in the herbs and sprinkle with a generous grating of black pepper.

Beetroot (Beet) and Potato Salad
··········

A Greek salad best enjoyed in early spring when the shoots of edible weeds and herbs appear, coinciding with the first crop of new potatoes from the garden, and one that few tourists have the good fortune to encounter. It is best to leave the potatoes whole, the highly nutritious skins intact. If available, fresh beetroot will have to be boiled for 30 minutes, but the more common cooked roots available in supermarkets may also be used.

675g/1½lb young fresh or cooked beetroot
675g/1½lb new potatoes
2 sticks of celery, washed
selection of edible weeds or fresh herbs
(rocket, young dandelion leaves, parsley, etc.)
very fruity or extra virgin olive oil
red wine vinegar
1 clove of garlic, peeled and finely chopped
salt

Boil the fresh beetroot in salted water until cooked, about 30 minutes. Boil the potatoes separately, until soft. Drain and cool these two vegetables in a pan of cold water. Remove and pat them dry. Peel and slice the beetroot thinly.

Slice the celery horizontally into thin strips.

Combine the vegetables and greens in a bowl and dress them with the oil and vinegar, to taste. Mix in the chopped garlic and season with the salt.

SALAD OF NEW POTATOES AND JERUSALEM (ROOT) ARTICHOKES

· · · · · · · · · ·

The point of this extremely healthy salad is to contrast textures, flavours and colours: soft new potatoes with crunchy raw carrot and Jerusalem artichoke; dark green, astringent spinach leaves with garlicky croûtons and crispy bacon. A good appetizer or, if the quantities are increased, a light meal in itself.

450g/1lb new potatoes, boiled until soft
110g/4oz fresh, tender spinach, washed and trimmed of stalks
2fl oz/4 tbs olive oil
4 slices of lean bacon, trimmed and cut into strips
1 clove of garlic, peeled
2 slices of bread, crusts removed, and diced
225g/8oz (peeled weight) Jerusalem artichokes, very thinly sliced
2 medium carrots, peeled and very thinly sliced
1$^1/_2$fl oz/3 tbs extra virgin olive oil
1 tbs balsamic or good wine vinegar
$^1/_2$ tsp grainy mustard
$^1/_2$ tsp sugar
salt
freshly milled black pepper

Ensure that the new potatoes and the spinach are completely dry.

Heat the oil in a small frying pan and sauté the bacon strips until they begin to brown. Reserve them. Add the garlic clove and allow it to colour slightly, then remove it. Quickly put in the bread and fry until crisp and golden. Remove and reserve it.

Combine the potatoes, spinach, Jerusalem artichokes and carrots in a salad bowl. Mix in the croûtons and bacon. Prepare the dressing by beating the extra virgin olive oil with the vinegar, mustard, sugar and seasoning. Pour over the salad, mix thoroughly and serve immediately.

THAI GREEN CHICKEN CURRY WITH NEW POTATOES
. . . .

Thai curry pastes can be made at home from fresh ingredients (see recipe below), or bought ready-made in jars, from Asian stores. They come in various forms, but the most commonly available are labelled 'red', and 'green'. If unavailable, fish sauce can be replaced with soy sauce.

1 chicken
350g/12oz new potatoes, washed
400ml/14fl oz can of coconut milk (unsweetened)
$^1/_2$ medium aubergine (eggplant), washed and cubed
2fl oz/4 tbs peanut oil
4cm/2 inch piece of fresh ginger, peeled and finely chopped
4 cloves of garlic, finely chopped
1tbs green curry paste
zest of $^1/_2$ lemon, or 1 lime
2–3 dried red chillies, crumbled
1fl oz/2 tbs Thai, Vietnamese or Filipino fish sauce
2 tsp sugar
heart of 1 lettuce, washed and shredded
1fl oz/2 tbs water
handful of basil

Bone and cut the chicken meat into strips or cubes. Simmer the chicken and the potatoes in the coconut milk for 15 minutes. Add the aubergines and continue to simmer for 10 more minutes.

Heat the peanut oil in a wok. Add the ginger, garlic and green curry paste and stir-fry for 2 minutes. Add the lemon zest, chillies, fish or soy sauce, sugar, then the mixture of coconut milk, potatoes and aubergines. Stir until the sauce thickens (3–4 minutes). Pour off any excess oil that may separate from the sauce, add the lettuce and the water. Garnish with the basil and serve with plain rice and sweet and sour carrot and cucumber relish.

Green curry paste

In a coffee grinder or mortar, grind 4 cloves, a small stick of cinnamon and 2 tsp each of cumin, caraway and coriander seeds, and black peppercorns.

Process to a paste with the following fresh ingredients: stick of lemon grass, or grated rind of a lime or ½ a lemon; 8 cloves of garlic, peeled; 2cm/1 inch piece of fresh galangal or ginger, peeled and sliced; 1 tsp shrimp paste; 2 tsp salt; 6 washed coriander (cilantro) roots and their leaves; 2fl oz/4tbs peanut oil; green chillies, to suit your own heat tolerance (Thais would use at least 8).

CURRY OF ROOT VEGETABLES

A warming curry of winter root vegetables and tubers that improves if re-heated the following day. Use a mixture of some or all of the following: potatoes, carrots, turnips, sweet potatoes, kohlrabi, celeriac (celery root), Jerusalem (root) artichokes, parsnips. Serve with a yoghurt *raita*, chutney and a *dal* or a fresh vegetable. Despite the abundance of starch, this is superb with plain rice.

800g/1³/₄lb mixed root vegetables, peeled
6 cloves of garlic, peeled and sliced
2cm/1 inch piece of fresh ginger, peeled and sliced
1 medium onion, peeled and chopped
2 large green chillies, washed and sliced

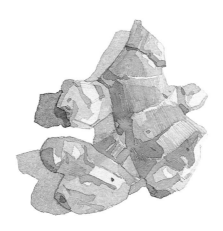

Garam masala made with:

4 cloves
1 tsp cumin seeds
2cm/1 inch stick of cinnamon
1 tsp fennel seeds
seeds from 1 tsp cardamom pods
2 tsp coriander seeds

2fl oz/4 tbs corn oil
2 tsp turmeric powder
4 canned tomatoes, crushed
560ml/1 pint water
2 bay leaves
salt

Cut the vegetables into 2cm/1 inch cubes.

Process the garlic, ginger, onion and chillies to a paste with 1fl oz/2 tbs of water in a food processor. Make the *garam masala* by pounding the dry spices in a pestle and mortar, or grind them in a clean coffee grinder.

Heat the oil in a large saucepan. Add the garlic, onion, chilli and ginger paste and fry for 4 minutes, stirring. Add half of the *garam masala* and the turmeric. Stir and fry for 1 minute more.

Add the vegetables, tomatoes, remaining water and bay leaves, and season with salt. Bring to a vigorous boil. Reduce, cover and simmer for 20 minutes. Then uncover, add the remaining *garam masala* and simmer for 10 more minutes. Serve.

MIXED GRATIN
· · · · · · · · · ·

Serve this delicious gratin as an appetizer, or even as a light lunch or supper, with a suitable salad. Use a mixture of roots and tubers, including celeriac (celery root), sweet potato and potatoes.

a little oil
2fl oz/4 tbs olive oil, plus a little more for dressing the gratin
1 medium onion, peeled and chopped
225g/8oz chanterelles, oyster, shiitake, or button mushrooms, sliced
4 cloves of garlic, peeled and chopped
generous handful of fresh parsley, washed and chopped
salt
freshly milled black pepper
225ml/8fl oz/1 cup dry white wine
675g/1½lb of roots and tubers, peeled and very thinly sliced
175g/6oz grated mature cheddar or gruyère cheese

Lightly oil a deep-sided baking dish. Pre-heat the oven to 200°C/400°F/gas mark 6.

Heat the olive oil in a frying pan and add the onion and mushrooms. Sauté over a high heat for 5–6 minutes, add half the chopped garlic, the parsley and season. Add half of the wine and boil it off, stirring well. Spoon a thin layer of the mixture into the dish.

Arrange the root and tuber slices over the mushroom layer, alternating and overlapping them slightly. Sprinkle with a little garlic, moisten with wine and a few drops of olive oil and top with grated cheese. Season lightly. Repeat the process, reserving some cheese to finish. Bake for 35 minutes, or until soft and golden.

GRATIN DAUPHINOIS
• • • • • • • • • •

This can be either an elegant appetizer or an accompaniment to a main course. It is important to slice the potatoes thinly and evenly. Although traditionally made with cream, you can substitute milk. For best results, use waxy potatoes such as Carlingford or all-purpose main crop potatoes.

675g/1½lb potatoes, peeled
oil
2 cloves of garlic, peeled and very finely chopped
1 tbs fresh parsley, washed and chopped
175g/6oz piece of parmesan, cheddar or gruyère, grated
225ml/8fl oz/1 cup milk
salt
freshly milled black pepper
small piece of nutmeg

Pre-heat an oven to 200°C/400°F/gas mark 6.

With a very sharp knife, slice the potatoes very thinly. Oil a baking dish and arrange a layer of potatoes to cover the bottom of the dish. Sprinkle with a little garlic, parsley and cheese and dribble with just enough milk to moisten. Season with salt, pepper and a grating of nutmeg. Repeat until the ingredients are used up. Bake for 45 minutes, until golden.

BASHED NEEPS

The Scots call swedes (rutabaga) 'neeps', although one would imagine the word is an abbreviation of turnip or parsnip. Traditionally, bashed neeps are served with haggis.

675g/1½lb swedes, peeled
50g/2oz butter
1 tsp sugar
salt
350ml/12fl oz/1½ cups water
freshly milled black pepper
a little grated nutmeg
2fl ozs/4tbs milk

Chop or slice the swedes and put them in a pot with half of the butter, the sugar and salt. Pour in the water, cover, and bring to the boil. Reduce to a gentle simmer and cook slowly for about 45 minutes. Uncover and pour off any water that may remain. Mash very thoroughly with a hand masher, adding the remaining butter, plenty of black pepper, some gratings of nutmeg and the milk. A prolonged 'bashing' should give a pleasantly fluffy result.

An excellent variation is 'neeps and tatties': follow the same recipe but drop in 450g/1lb of peeled, diced potatoes halfway through the boiling time for the swedes. Proceed as above.

PUREE OF CELERIAC (CELERY ROOT)

a small celeriac, peeled and chopped
2 medium potatoes, peeled and chopped
salt
freshly milled black pepper
small piece of nutmeg
110ml/4fl oz/$\frac{1}{2}$ cup live, strained yoghurt, well beaten
25g/1oz butter

Bring a large pot of salted water to the boil with the
chopped vegetables. Boil them for 30 minutes, then
drain them well, pouring all the water away. Return
them to the pan and start mashing the vegetables with
a hand masher. Season well and add a few gratings of
nutmeg, to taste. When thoroughly smooth, fold in the
yoghurt and butter and serve at once. This will com-
plement most stews or saucy main course dishes.

You can also make fritters with any leftovers by
following the method for potato croquettes, adding
flour, some parmesan cheese and seasoning to the
purée, shaping it into croquettes and frying them in oil.

Ensaladilla Rusa

This very appealing salad of potatoes, carrots and peas dressed with mayonnaise is far less 'Russian' than Latin: it is popular in Italy and Spain, where it is often known simply as *ensaladilla* (little salad), and where it is to be sampled in any *cervecería*, or beer bar. Huge quantities are forked on to bread and washed down with excellent draught beer. Use varieties of potato best suited to boiling, or general-purpose potatoes. Serve with a selection of hors d'oeuvres, including some cured ham.

1 small or ½ a red pepper
4–6 medium carrots, peeled
900g/2lb waxy potatoes
150g/5oz peas (thawed, if frozen)
2fl oz/4 tbs extra virgin olive oil
1fl oz/2 tbs red wine vinegar
a little fresh parsley, washed and finely chopped
2 tsp salt
freshly milled black pepper
pinch of cayenne
225ml/8fl oz/1 cup home-made mayonnaise

Grill (broil) the red pepper until the skin blisters and blackens. Cover and let it cool.

Meanwhile bring a pot of water to the boil and put in the carrots and the potatoes. Cover and boil until the vegetables are just soft, adding the peas to cook for the last few minutes. Drain, plunge them into cold water to cool and dice the carrots and potatoes finely (you can peel the potatoes or leave the skins on if they are thin).

In a bowl beat the oil, vinegar, parsley and seasonings together and mix thoroughly. Add the vegetables and fold in the mayonnaise.

Transfer to a shallow serving dish and press the mixture down with the back of a spoon, to level it.

Remove the skins, pith and seeds from the peppers and finely shred the flesh. Sprinkle over the salad. Keep for an hour before serving, to allow the flavours to develop. This will also keep for two or three days in the fridge, covered.

Hashed Brown, Rösti Potatoes
. . . .

Similar to Swiss *rösti* potatoes, hash browns are an American classic, and are superb with eggs. Olive oil replaces butter in this recipe but the results are no worse for that. Suitable varieties include, Catriona , King Edward , and Pentland Hawk , Ivory or Squire . 'Hashed' means finely chopped or grated.

2fl oz/4 tbs olive oil
4 slices of lean bacon, trimmed and diced small
675g 1½lb potatoes, peeled and coarsely grated
salt
freshly milled black pepper
pinch of dried thyme (optional)

Heat the olive oil in a large, well seasoned or non-stick frying pan and add the bacon. When crisp and brown, remove it and put in the potatoes. Stir for 1 minute to coat with oil, then season well with salt, pepper and thyme (if using), reduce the heat and cover the pan. Without stirring, let the potatoes cook until they are soft (about 15 minutes) then remove the cover and raise the heat. Cook for 1 minute more to form a brown crust on the base, loosen the bottom, and invert on to a plate with any scraps. Sprinkle the bacon over the potatoes. Serve very hot.

To cook a Swiss *rösti*, prepare the same quantity of potatoes and substitute a medium, chopped onion for the bacon, but keep it in the pan with the potatoes. Season well and lightly brown the potatoes by stirring them around for 10 minutes before flattening the potatoes in the pan to make a cake. Cook for 5 more minutes to form a crust. Add a little chopped fresh parsley.

ROAST POTATOES AND PARSNIPS

Perfect, crisp roast potatoes are guaranteed if four simple rules are observed: first, they must be of a variety that is suitable for roasting, such as Catriona, Desirée, Golden Wonder, Estima, Maris Piper and Record; secondly, they must be par-boiled; thirdly, the peeled surfaces must be roughened to encourage the formation of a crust; and finally, the oven must be very hot. Roast parsnips are deliciously sweet and require a little less cooking and none of the preparatory measures just mentioned: just add them approximately half way through the cooking time.

1 kg/2¼lb potatoes, peeled
6–8 parsnips, scrubbed with a sharp blade
110ml/4fl oz/½ cup sunflower, corn or olive oil

Pre-heat an oven to 230°C/450°F/Gas Mark 8.

Halve the potatoes, unless they are on the small side. Cut the parsnips into chunks. Bring a large pot of water to the boil and drop in the potatoes. Boil for 10 minutes, then remove and drain them.

When they are cool enough to touch, score the potatoes all over with a fork. Put them in a large, wide baking pan and dribble the oil over them, turning them so they are well coated. Put them into the oven, and after 30 minutes, reduce the heat to moderate (190°C/375°F/gas mark 5), and add the parsnips, coating them well with the oil. Return and roast for 30–40 minutes longer. Check that the parsnips are soft, transfer to a serving dish and serve.

BAKED SWEET POTATOES

Not to be confused with yams, red-skinned sweet potatoes are the edible tuber of a convolvulus plant native to Central America and are quite unrelated to 'true' potatoes. They are the starchy staple in many tropical countries, although in China, they are considered fit only for animals, no doubt because rice is the universal staple there. Like carrots, their yellow flesh is a good source of beta carotene, the form of vitamin A that appears to provide some protection against certain cancers. Here, their natural sweetness is contrasted with a tangy filling.

2 large sweet potatoes
110g/4oz cream cheese
2 tbs fresh chives and parsley, washed and chopped
tiny pinch of cayenne
salt
freshly milled black pepper

Pre-heat an oven to 200°C/400°F/gas mark 6. Bake the sweet potatoes for 1¼ hours, or until the skin rises up from the flesh in pockets.

Meanwhile, mash the cream cheese with the herbs and seasoning. When the potatoes are soft, remove them and slice them open. Spread each inner surface with a layer of the cream cheese mixture and serve with a leafy salad. Alternatively, scoop out the flesh and mash it with the mixture.

Some other cooking suggestions for sweet potatoes include boiling and puréeing them with a little sugar and milk; roasting; boiling and serving them in sour cream heated through with paprika; and the popular American method of par-boiling and slicing, then 'candying' them in an oven, sprinkled with brown sugar or maple syrup and orange or lemon juice.

STIR-FRIED KOHLRABI

Although not strictly a root because the swollen edible ball develops just above the soil, kohlrabi are greatly appreciated in eastern Europe and in various parts of Asia. They make an excellent stir-fry, combined with carrots, or may be braised or curried. Oyster sauce is available in Oriental stores.

3 kohlrabi, peeled
3 medium carrots, peeled
2fl oz/4 tbs peanut oil
3 cloves of garlic, peeled and thinly sliced
2cm/1 inch piece of ginger root, peeled and thinly sliced
3 spring onions (scallions), washed and sliced
1–2 fresh chilli peppers, washed, peeled and sliced
110ml/4fl oz/$^1/_2$ cup water
salt
2fl oz/4 tbs oyster sauce

Cube the kohlrabi and carrots and slice each piece diagonally in thin sections, to produce flat elongated ovals.

Heat the peanut oil in a wok, and when it smokes, throw in the garlic and ginger. Stir once and add the vegetables. Toss them around for 2 minutes, then add the spring onions and chilli peppers. Stir-fry for another minute, then pour in the water. Cover, reduce the heat and cook for 5 minutes. Remove the cover, add a little salt and the oyster sauce. Toss briefly to glaze the vegetables, and serve.

SRI OWEN'S INDONESIAN FRUIT AND VEGETABLE SALAD
·········

The white winter radish is a large, heavy root vegetable very closely related to the Japanese daikon (other names for these radishes are mooli and icicle radish). In this traditional Indonesian recipe, it is served raw and retains its radishy taste. (Ordinary small red or white radishes can be substituted.) Serve the salad before, with, or after a main course.

1fl oz/2 tbs rice vinegar
1 tsp sugar
2 tsp salt
pinch of cayenne
1 tbs water
$\frac{1}{2}$ cucumber, peeled
2 medium, hard apples, peeled, cored and thinly sliced
4 leaves of white cabbage, finely shredded
1 large white radish, or 6 small red or white radishes,
thinly sliced
2 carrots, peeled and cut into matchsticks

Prepare the dressing by mixing together the vinegar, sugar, salt, cayenne and water.

Halve the cucumber vertically, scoop out the seeds and slice it into very thin semicircles. Put the apples and vegetables into a salad bowl. Pour the dressing over them, mix well and let the salad stand for at least an hour. Toss and turn it from time to time.

BEEF STEW WITH TURNIPS

A really satisfying *daube* for late winter and early spring that may be made in advance and re-heated; indeed, the flavour improves if served the next day. Serve with steaming mounds of fluffy potato mashed with a little milk and extra virgin olive oil. Look for good quality, lean cuts of stewing beef such as the tail end of rump.

1125g/2¹/₂lb stewing beef, trimmed of all fat and gristle
3fl oz/6 tbs olive oil
2 large onions, peeled and chopped
4 slices of bacon, trimmed and diced
1 large carrot, peeled and chopped
1 stick of celery, washed and sliced
6 cloves of garlic, peeled and chopped
560ml/1 pint red wine
2 fl oz/4 tbs water
2 tbs tomato paste
some sprigs of thyme and parsley and 2 bay leaves
a long strip of orange peel
6–8 medium or small turnips, peeled and quartered
salt and freshly milled black pepper

Cut the beef evenly into chunks about 3cm/1¹/₄ inch square.

Heat the olive oil and brown the meat in it. Remove it and lightly brown the onions. Then add the bacon, to brown, followed by the carrots, celery and garlic. Return the meat, pour in the red wine and water, adding the tomato paste. Stir well, put in the herbs and orange peel, and cover.

Reduce the heat to very low and simmer gently for 1 hour. Put in the turnips, season and simmer for another 1¹/₄ hours. Remove the hard thyme stalks, bay leaves and orange peel and serve.

PICKLED WINTER VEGETABLES

S tart preparing these sweet, hot and sour 'pickled' vegetables 2 hours before you eat and serve them as an hors d'oeuvre or appetizer. Substitute ordinary red radishes for mooli which can be hard to find, but do not peel them.

450g/1lb carrots, peeled
225g/8oz Jerusalem (root) artichokes, peeled
1 long white winter radish, or mooli, peeled
50g/2oz sugar
$^{1}/_{2}$ tsp salt
2fl oz/4 tbs rice vinegar
2 dried red chillies, crumbled

Slice the carrots and Jerusalem artichokes thinly across the diagonal. Cut the radishes into 1cm/$^{1}/_{2}$ inch cubes. If using common radishes, trim them but leave them whole.

Combine the vegetables in a bowl. Stir the sugar, salt and rice vinegar together until the sugar has dissolved and pour the mixture over the vegetables. Mix in the chillies, cover and keep for 2 hours in the fridge, stirring occasionally. Serve.

SWEET AND SOUR CARROT AND CUCUMBER RELISH
· · · · · · · · · ·

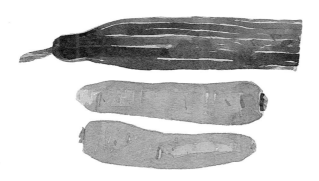

This Thai-style relish is particularly good with spicy chicken kebabs.

2 medium carrots scrubbed, halved and thinly sliced
$^1/_2$ cucumber, peeled, washed, and halved
2 tbs sugar
1fl oz/2 tbs rice vinegar
2–3 dried red chillies, crumbled
2 spring onions (scallions) washed and sliced
handful of coriander (cilantro), washed and chopped
75g/3 oz peanuts, crushed

Remove the seedy centre from the cucumber with a teaspoon. Slice the cucumber thinly.

Put the carrots and cucumber in a bowl. Combine the sugar and vinegar in a small pan, bring to the boil, and simmer for 5 minutes. Allow to cool a little before pouring over the vegetables. Sprinkle with chillies, spring onions, coriander and peanuts.

CURRIED PARSNIP SOUP
· · · · · · · · · ·

A very pleasant soup that is best served hot. Avoid commercial stock (broth) cubes but try to find good quality liquid stock, or make your own, following the recipes in this book.

2fl oz/4 tbs olive oil
1 onion, peeled and chopped
6–8 parsnips, peeled and chopped
white parts of 2 leeks, washed and chopped
2 carrots, peeled and chopped
stick of celery, washed and chopped
1 medium potato, peeled and diced
1 1/2 tbs *garam masala*
1 tsp cayenne
2 bay leaves
salt
1 3/4 litres/3 pints of vegetable stock (broth)
2fl oz/4 tbs crème fraîche (optional)
handful of coriander (cilantro), washed and chopped

Make the vegetable stock or have the bought stock ready.

Heat the oil in a large pot and, stirring often, soften the onions over a low heat, without burning them (about 8 minutes). Add the other vegetables and sauté for 5 minutes before adding the *garam masala* (see the curry recipe), cayenne, bay leaves and salt. Increase the heat and brown everything for 3–4 minutes before pouring in the stock. Bring to the boil, cover, reduce the heat and simmer until the vegetables are soft (about 30 minutes).

Remove the bay leaves, cool and process the contents in a food processor. Return the soup to the pan, and re-heat thoroughly, without boiling, before transferring it to a tureen. Stir in the crème fraîche (if using), re-season with salt, if necessary, and garnish with the coriander.

Soupe au Pistou

A tasty Provençal soup of potatoes, pasta and butter beans, enriched with fragrant *pistou* (pesto). Use the smaller types of pasta designed especially for soups, such as *farfallini*, *stellini*, or *vermicelli*.

500g/18oz dried butter beans
450g/1lb potatoes, peeled and diced
4 canned or fresh tomatoes, peeled and chopped
225g/8oz factory-made pasta
salt
freshly milled black pepper
1 1/2 loosely packed cups of fresh basil leaves
3 cloves of garlic, peeled and chopped
1 tsp salt
3fl oz/6 tbs extra virgin olive oil
50g/2oz piece of parmesan, grated

Soak the beans overnight in plenty of water. Drain them.

Bring 3 1/2 litres/6 1/4 pints of salted water to the boil in a large pot. Add the potatoes, beans and tomatoes and simmer them for 1 1/2 hours. Stir in the pasta and simmer for 8–10 minutes longer, or until the pasta is cooked, stirring occasionally. Season well.

Meanwhile, prepare the *pistou* by pounding or processing the basil, garlic, 1 tsp salt and olive oil. Stir this into the soup and simmer for a minute longer. Serve with grated parmesan cheese.

BARSCH

This very refined Polish beetroot (beet) consommé is always served on Christmas Eve (the feast of Wigilia), along with such meatless delicacies as marinated herrings with soured cream, carp, and various salads. It is a beautiful ruby colour and unlike Ukrainian borscht, this is a strained soup, to which the vegetables, the dried ceps especially, contribute their colour and flavour but are absent from the soup itself. It is served with little mushroom-filled dumplings. Resist the temptation to use pre-cooked beetroot: only fresh will do.

575g/1¼lb fresh beetroot, sliced
1 small celeriac (celery root), peeled and sliced
1½ litres/2¾ pints home-made vegetable stock (broth)
1 onion, peeled and halved
2 cloves of garlic, peeled
4–6 parsley stalks, with leaves attached
25g/1oz dried ceps (*boletus edulis, porcini*)
juice of a ½ lemon
2 tsp sugar
salt

Combine everything except the lemon juice, sugar and salt in a pot, cover, and simmer for an hour. Strain into another pot and add the flavourings. Remove and reserve the mushrooms. Re-heat gently and serve hot with mushroom dumplings.

Mushroom dumplings

220g/7oz/1¼ cups plain (all-purpose) flour
2 eggs
½ tsp salt
1fl oz/2 tbs olive oil
1 small onion, peeled and chopped
the wild mushrooms used to flavour the barsch
175g/6oz wild or cultivated mushrooms, diced
generous handful each of fresh parsley and dill, washed
salt
freshly milled black pepper

In a food processor, blend the flour, eggs and salt briefly. The dough should roll up into a ball. Let it rest for 15 minutes, then roll it out thinly on a floured work surface. Cut the sheet into 4cm/2 inch squares.

Heat the oil in a small pan and add the onion. Soften it for a few minutes, then add the mushrooms. Sauté over high heat for 6–8 minutes, then add the parsley and dill. Season and remove. When the mixture has cooled a little, spoon a little mound into the centres of the squares of dough. Pinch the edges together, moistening them with a little water. Ensure that all edges are sealed.

Bring a large pot of water to the boil and simmer the dumplings for 6–8 minutes. Drain and serve them in the soup bowl, ladling the barsch over them.

POTATO CROQUETTES

Potato croquettes are popular home-made fare in Italy and Greece and doubtless in other southern European countries too. They are made with mashed potato and another, strongly flavoured ingredient such as spring onions (scallions) or cured ham. Serve alone, or as an accompaniment to a main course.

675g/1¹/₂lb baking potatoes, peeled
1¹/₂fl oz/3 tbs olive oil
some gratings of nutmeg
salt
freshly milled black pepper
2 eggs
50g/2oz piece of parmesan, grated
110g/4oz cured ham, diced small *or*
2 spring onions, washed and chopped
generous handful of parsley, washed and chopped
175g/6oz/1 scant cup of flour
olive oil for frying

Boil the potatoes in plenty of water and when soft, drain and mash them with 1½fl oz/3 tbs of olive oil and a few gratings of nutmeg. Season well.

Beat the eggs and mix in the parmesan, ham (or spring onions) and parsley. Add to the mashed potatoes, and combine everything thoroughly. Add half of the flour and mix again. Allow the mixture to cool until comfortable enough to handle.

Pour some of the remaining flour onto a work surface and with floured hands shape the mixture into small balls, rolling them in the flour. Roll each into small sausage shapes and dust with more flour.

Heat plenty of olive oil in a well seasoned or non-stick frying pan. When it starts to smoke, carefully put in the fragile croquettes, in batches, without crowding the pan. Turn them to brown evenly and drain on paper towel. Serve hot.

Aloo kofta

The spicy Indian version of potato croquettes is just as delicious. Proceed as above but omit the olive oil when mashing, adding ½ tsp cayenne, 1½ tsp of *garam masala* and substituting fresh coriander (cilantro) for the bacon or spring onions (scallions). Omit also the parsley and cheese but otherwise, proceed as above, replacing the olive oil with a light vegetable oil when frying. Serve hot.

Apopular *tapa* from Spain, the name of which translates as 'fierce potatoes'. Untamed ferocity is a quality that is much admired in fighting bulls, and the eponymous coastline of the north eastern corner of Spain was once untamed and rugged, before it was developed for tourism. Here the term reflects the heat of the chillies and the angry red colour of the potatoes. Use general-purpose potatoes or varieties best suited to frying and roasting.

2fl oz/4 tbs hot water
pinch of saffron strands
900g/2lb potatoes, peeled
2fl oz/4 tbs olive oil
2 cloves of garlic, peeled and finely chopped
1 medium onion, peeled and finely chopped
2–3 dried red chilli peppers, crumbled, or $\frac{1}{2}$ tsp cayenne
200g/7oz canned plum tomatoes, crushed
pinch of sugar
bay leaf
1 tbs paprika
olive oil, for frying the potatoes
salt
freshly milled black pepper
handful of fresh parsley, washed and chopped

Soak the saffron in the hot water.

Cut the potatoes evenly into cubes of about $1\frac{1}{2}$cm/ $\frac{3}{4}$ inch.

Start on the sauce: heat 2fl oz/4 tbs of the oil in a pan, add the garlic and onion and sauté them until soft, then add the chillies, tomatoes, sugar, bay leaf, saffron and its soaking liquid, and paprika. Cover and cook to reduce a little, about 15 minutes. (The sauce should not dry out.)

Meanwhile, heat olive oil in another pan and put in the potatoes. Cover and cook them over low heat until soft (about 10 minutes). Remove the cover and increase the heat, to brown (5 more minutes). Finish the sauce and potatoes by seasoning both. Combine the two in a serving dish and sprinkle with parsley. Serve hot.

STOCK (BROTH)

Because some of the recipes in this book call for home-made stock, here are two simple recipes, one for chicken, the other for vegetable stock.

1 uncooked, skinned chicken carcass
2 large onions, peeled and quartered
2 large carrots, peeled and roughly chopped
1 large stick of celery, roughly chopped
bunch of fresh parsley (stalks and leaves)
12 black peppercorns
2 bay leaves
salt
2 litres/3$\frac{1}{2}$ pints water

Put all the ingredients into a very large pot and bring to a boil. Cover, reduce the heat and simmer, skimming off the scum from time to time. After 2 hours, the stock will be ready. Allow it to cool, remove any surplus fat and refrigerate or pour into freezer bags and store in the freezer until required. To thaw, pour boiling water over the frozen stock and carefully peel away the bag. Put the block of frozen stock into a pot, cover and simmer until completely melted.

To make vegetable stock, combine in a large pot 2fl oz/4 tbs of olive oil, 2 peeled onions, 2–3 leeks, 3 carrots, 5–6 celery stalks, a parsnip, 2 tomatoes, some parsley stalks with their leaves, 1 tbs tomato paste, salt, freshly milled black pepper, and 2 litres/3$\frac{1}{2}$ pints of water. Bring to the boil, stir well, cover, reduce the heat and simmer for 1$\frac{1}{2}$ hours. Re-season. Store as above.

CARROT CAKE

A classic cake with a moist texture and spicy flavour that is so easy as to appeal even to the greenest novice. It may be frosted if so desired.

225g/8oz carrots, peeled and grated
110ml/4fl oz/$^1/_2$ cup light seed or sunflower oil
110g/4oz brown sugar
2 tbs honey
2 eggs, beaten
2 tsp ground cinnamon
a little grated nutmeg
175g/6oz/1 cup of plain (all-purpose) flour
1 tsp bicarbonate of soda (baking soda)
$^1/_2$ tsp salt

Pre-heat an oven to 175°C/350°F/gas mark 4.

Line a round cake tin (pan) with buttered grease-proof (waxed) paper.

Combine the carrots with the oil, sugar, honey and eggs. Mix well. Sift the spices with the flour and bicarbonate of soda, add the salt, and combine thoroughly with the first mixture. Pour into the cake tin, spread evenly and bake for an hour or until a fork comes out cleanly. Cool on a wire rack.